OUTFLANKING POPULISM

A Manifesto to Inspire Trust, to Create Hope, and Demand Immediate Positive Change

George Evans

Published by Bite-Sized Books Limited 2025
16 High Holborn, London, WC1V 6BX England
Registered in the UK. Company Registration
No: 9395379

ISBN: 978-1-0682808-2-5

Cover image: 1896 *Judge* cartoon shows
William Jennings Bryan/Populism as a snake swallowing up the mule representing the Democratic party.

Frontispiece

© Denis Lushch Victoria, Australia

Contents

Introduction

This isn't a time for words – words are drowned out by the offshore billionaire press and the cacophony of voices on offshore billionaire-owned social media. This is a time for action – for immediate action by the Labour Government, and by Labour MPs who are discovering their backbone and taking on blue Labour.

It's so easy to be outraged by populism and populists – the lies, the half truths, the apparently easy answers, the deflections, the contempt for the rule of law, the polarisation of society, the complete lack of empathy and the focus on division and setting people against people. One high profile populist has justified the lies during the Brexit campaign by saying that the Remain side lied too. What does that say about our country and our politicians? It is no wonder that so many people have lost faith in governments and think they should give the populists a try.

The UK is a rich country but the wealth is concentrated in so few hands now that most people feel that it is what Yanis Varoufakis calls an *assetocracy*. The extraordinarily rich people, with more money than they could spend in a lifetime, own our lives and are intent on keeping all the money for themselves.

There is no doubt that fury with the establishment is one of the driving forces in our society and for good reason. For the reasons I will go on to cover in Chapter 1, we – that is all of us not part of the establishment – are rightly angry with what they have done to our country and our society. The populists – to a person part of the establishment – have cleverly and cynically diverted that fury towards minorities: immigrants, Muslims, Jews, people on benefits, anyone who isn't *us* – whatever that means in *Daily Mail* land.

Outrage and attacks on the populists are completely self-defeating. Yes – there are some very unpleasant people forcing the populist agenda, supported by the richest people in the world, mostly covertly, but we need to outflank them and address the real issues that are hurting ordinary people, and where the populists are sowing division and hate, create unity and hope.

Not all supporters of populists are fascists – and that is an important point. (Though it is true that all fascists are populists.)

Many of the people tempted by populism are at the end of their tether – quite rightly. Fourteen years of corruption and attacks on the living standards of the less well off by the Tories have created a perfect seed bed for the populists to exploit. The arrival of Starmer's blue Labour, wedded to austerity and outmoded fiscal rules and without a vision of how to create a sensible inclusive society, has only exacerbated that despair amongst ordinary people and a feeling that no-one is on *our* side.

It was always going to happen, once Starmer repudiated *all* the promises he made to become leader of the Labour Party, so it is no surprise but now we need to change our politics – and not, as the populists want, by, for example, abolishing the NHS, creating more antidemocratic so-called *Special Economic Zones* (SEZs) and so-called *Freeports*, and carrying on with the same old heavy taxes on less well-off people.

We have already seen what the populists will do if we give them any political power. In Lancashire the Reform-led council has already decided to have cuts in early years education – hurting the very people who presumably voted for them. That wasn't part of any manifesto. They keep stum about what they will do. Richard Tice has already supported the promise by the Reform Lincolnshire council to oppose solar farms. Just straws in the wind – but we need to make sure that people understand what Reform really stands for.

Apart from those of us who thought that Starmer would be disastrous and would immediately introduce just slightly less bad Tory policies, did anyone imagine that the first targets of a new Labour Government, elected with an enormous majority, would be to take winter fuel payments from pensioners and means test them and reduce the support for disabled people? How crass – and how much that plays into the populists' hands and their cry *they're all the same*.

The problem is that at the moment they are.

I wouldn't trust Starmer's political judgment ever, but now he is proving disastrous and actually creating the seedbed for the success of the populists. The surge in support for the populists is precisely because Starmer and Reeves are pursuing exactly the same policies as the Tories and driving people away from Labour. All Labour MPS who were freshly elected in 2024 must feel they are vulnerable – so now is the time to make sure they discover their power and take on blue Labour.

The approach must be to do what is required – actually lots of things – that improve people's lives immediately and at the same time create a complete narrative based on facts and those actual changes that affect us – the ordinary people – and to present a positive, united vision underpinned by real improvements in people's lived experience and create a sense of solidarity against the malign forces of the rich and powerful.

We must bring people together, focus on the real issues and present a vision of the future that will unite and avoid going down the rabbit holes of deflection so cleverly used by the populists.

In short a new settlement, like the post-Second World War settlement.

That settlement created the National Health Service, nationalised the railways, provided education that didn't just serve industry but enhanced people's lives with literature, music and discovery, developed social services and a welfare state that said an injury to one of us is an injury to all of us.

This new dynamic settlement has to be properly supportive of all people, not just the rich and powerful, the tax dodgers, the offshore billionaires controlling our political narrative, the offshore billionaires laundering their money through London, often by buying properties forcing up our house prices, the bankers funding drug and people trafficking cartels, the corrupt hangers on. For too long they have avoided prison, avoided tax, placed their money offshore so it was hidden (see the *Panama Papers*), and binged on our money through immediate programmes like the *Troubled Asset Relief Programme* (TARP) and *Quantitative Easing* (a phrase that covers up a lot of corruption). The bankers were initially prevented from taking bonuses, but it didn't mean that they couldn't increase their salaries – which they did.

People are crying out for change – and both Tories and Labour are continuing the *same old, same old* which has failed every ordinary person in the UK. No wonder a promise of real change by the populists – never mind it will hurt the very people being persuaded to vote for it – is attractive.

The Labour Government is constantly watering down its commitment to people – notice the way that Starmer constantly talks about helping, not all of us, but just *working people.* He is deliberately further dividing and standardising an under-class when he should be building solidarity and unity. He talks of change but in reality he is destroying the foundations of our democracy.

Apparently to pay for killing foreigners – that is the Defence budget increase – Starmer and Reeves reduced the amount we spend on foreign aid by 40% from 0.5% of GDP to 0.3% of GDP – which will hit the poorest people in the world. And this a Labour Government! It is the type of thing we expect from the Tories. The populists love this of course – and it creates disaffection in the Labour voting community, which then despairs of seeing any genuine humanity in Starmer.

Make no mistake, if elected, just as Trump is destroying the US Constitution, the populists will immediately ride rough shod over all of our institutions. The right to protest, already severely limited by the

Tories and not even worried about by Labour, is being undermined now – but in future as the courts are prevented from exercising their oversight of illegal government action, our whole democracy, for what it is worth now, will be gone..

Tackling the populists head on is a losing strategy – they have complete control over the media and communications so we are drowned out by the evangelicals of hate.

People don't necessarily remember the fact that fifty years ago one earner in a family could support that family and an increasing standard of living, whereas now this is impossible. Property prices forced up by the non-doms living virtually tax free at our expense, laundering their money, have made the idea of owning your own home impossible for Gen Z, many of whom are mired in debt because of university fees. At the same time, the ratio of chief executive salary, before bonuses, to the lowest paid employee is something like a minimum of 300 to one, as opposed to then when it was 40 to 1.

The BBC is caught up in this promotion of populists with its so-called *balanced view* – equal time is given to research based on the scientific work of, say, climate scientists, and a person who doesn't believe there is climate change, and equal time is given to people who can prove that vaccines have saved millions of lives and self-styled antivaxxers who think otherwise for whatever malign reason, then extra time is given to the populists on programmes like *Question Time* with its rigged audience – the BBC admitted it biased the audience towards the Tories when they were in government.

The populists have two weapons that they deploy initially and so effectively, dividing us and setting ordinary people against ordinary people.

The first is deflection – *look at that person over there who is not like you and is a threat to your job and livelihood* but all the while corporates and their executives are stealing money from us, whether it is the so-called *Quantitative* Easing – giving money to rich bankers - or the Covid procurement scandals.

Deflection is coupled with wilful blindness – *we can't see that there is anything wrong and so we needn't do anything about it* while refusing to investigate the awful tragedies exposed by, for example, the Post Office scandal, the Grenfell cladding disaster or the CJE blood scandal. Immediately the government – any government – will promise instant action and wait for the fuss to die down, before doing absolutely nothing. This is then doubled down on with hypocritical and spurious deflecting arguments: *if you criticise the state of Israel over what it is doing in Gaza that's antisemitism.*

The second weapon they deploy is overt and covert division, building on deflection and wilful blindness – *train drivers are earning far more than you and they are holding the country to ransom, and that's why train fares are astronomical.*

So how do we counter that? Not by saying – *if I were holding the country to ransom, I wouldn't settle for a 5% pay increase.* And who could we say it too?

Our task then is to mobilise opinion where we can but realise this is a thankless and ultimately fruitless task without direct improvements in people's lives as the rich and powerful will control the Overton Window – that is what is considered worthwhile discussing – and outrage will prove nugatory. With over 80% of the media owned by offshore millionaires and billionaires, the chances of getting that message across are slim. People point to the power of the social media platforms as channels to creating the new narrative. But this is only a small part of the way forward. The trouble is that with the way the tech billionaires control social media, that it is allowing as much diversity of opinion, conspiracy theories and prejudice as possible, and with no moderation at all, it just becomes a cacophony. Of course this is aided by the fact that most of the internet that they control is deliberately anonymous so people feel emboldened to write things that they probably wouldn't put their real names to. It creates a perfect storm. No message survives intact and people are bombarded with so many different opinions that in the end, no-one believes anyone.

As Hannah Arendt pointed out, referring to Hitler and Goebbels, they didn't lie to be believed – although any dimwits who believed what they said were a bonus – but in order to destroy any faith in anything that is said politically. Trump, Johnson, Farage and Modi have followed the same playbook and so many people will say they just can't believe anything politicians say, and for good reason – so they have won.

As I have said, there is enough for every person not a millionaire to be outraged about.

We will not outflank the populists with any messages, they are too powerful and too in control of all the media for that to be successful. We have to have action, actual physical and practical action that improves people's lives – and at the same time create a narrative that gives hope and creates unity.

My first chapter is a catalogue of some of the things that people are rightly angry about. It's not a short list. If your child cannot get a proper education suited to their needs, if you can't afford to live without getting in debt, if you can't get a place to live that is of a reasonable standard and you see the rich and famous cheating and defrauding us, no wonder you are outraged. When you know the government is lying to you and defrauding you, as I shall show in Chapter 1, and doing so as though it is not important, you are right to be outraged.

Because of the way Bite-Sized Books are produced, if you have further examples, then write to *information@bite-sizedbooks.com*, and they might be able to add them to Chapter 1.

The populists aren't feeding on nothing as these are real sores that hurt ordinary people every day.

The second chapter is a manifesto focused on what we need to do about each and every one of the scandals and lies, the fraud and the sleight of hand, the deflection and the hypocrisy, the way we are divided from each other. It is a long list and to some brought up on the gutter press – *The Times, The Daily Telegraph, The Sun, the Daily Mail, The Daily Express* – will seem too radical as it is radical and will restore the belief in ourselves and our society, not at the expense of minorities but at the expense of the oligarchs, the billionaires and the evil manipulators of information to protect themselves.

It requires real action immediately, backed up by the narrative of extolling our new settlement.

If you think about it, most people will know why the Tories increased VAT by 40% from 8% to 20% - it taxes disproportionately the less well off and allowed them to reduce the top rate of income tax by a third. Yet somehow, because of the complete control of the current narrative, people have stopped being outraged by it and they believe the Tories only increased the rate by 12%.

It is extraordinary to me that what we in the 60s and 70s thought of as centre left policies are now regarded by the establishment and the mainstream media as extreme. Who would have thought that providing water would have become a toy of greedy monopolists unchecked by any rules and this is accepted by a large proportion of the country?

The third chapter is focused on the real task which is to demand action, building on the manifesto for change – direct action now to improve people's lives and their perception of government, focusing on accountability and creating trust. The Labour Government, with its 166 seat majority needs to focus on righting the wrongs of the last fifteen years and Labour back benchers need to grow a spine – and there are signs that they are – and demand positive, progressive action on all our issues. We also need to build a movement to create the new settlement that puts the billionaires and the offshore tax dodgers in their place and restores the values of our society.

In Parliament there are 403 Labour MPs – well, that includes some of the ones Starmer has expelled for not voting for Tory policies. We need every one of the Labour back benchers to stand up and deliver this programme and reverse 46 years of decline in social cohesion and social consciousness. We know most of them have a conscience – many stood up to Reeves and Starmer – and we must motivate them. Many of them stand to lose their seats if they don't and that must be the greatest motivator of all. We must build on that great incentive.

No more can we sit idly by and think there are people of goodwill controlling our lives even though that is how they present themselves.

Just like that initial post Second World War generation, we have to insist that the people who have injured so many are brought to justice, but more than that, that people's lives are fundamentally changed for the better. We have to build this from the grass roots but we must do it and do it quickly. Arresting a banker for supporting the drug and people trafficking cartels would be a good start. We need positive action – and we need symbolic action like that to show we mean business.

Chapter 2 is the manifesto to create hope, instil trust once again in government and unify our country – getting rid of the deflection and absolute failure to improve ordinary people's lives.

Chapter 3 is focused on further actions to create hope and trust – and unify the country.

Chapter 4 is some further observations about the way we must change the country quickly and outflank the populists and their lies, deflections and secret money – and it will require all Labour MPs to remember the values of the Labour Party, reject the world of asset strippers, offshore billionaires and bankers who have enabled drug and people trafficking cartels.

It is a call for action. And it is action not words that will outflank the populists.

Chapter 1

The Misery, Corruption and Failures the Populists Exploit

Most people have a well-developed sense of fairness. It was that sense of fairness that drove the 1945-1951 Labour Government under Clement Attlee to create a fairer world buttressed by the fact that having fought tyranny the people of this country weren't going to settle for poverty and the empty promise that was given after World War 1 that there would a country fit for heroes.

Between 1945 and 1951, it was a world where Keynesian economics – stimulating the economy and ensuring that people are well paid and have an increasing standard of living – was proven to work and where austerity, taking money out of the economy just when it needed more money circulating, was shown to be self-defeating. Something that Cameron and Osborne proved once again between 2010 and 2015, when the national deficit went up while they were cynically cutting all social programmes, using austerity to reduce the support for ordinary people and direct more wealth to the already rich.

The accepted economics were based on the quantity of money in the economy when it was the speed of circulation that was the key to growth for ordinary people. Give money to the rich, as the Tories did, does nothing because they either squirrel it away in offshore tax havens or save it here. Ordinary people don't have that luxury and now with so many people *just about managing*, any money redistributed from the rich will be spent quickly – enhancing the economy.

It was a world in the 40s, 50, and 60s where the inequalities of wealth in this country were being reduced, unlike the last 46 years where wealth has been taken out of ordinary people's lives and given to the rich and powerful.

As a result, the populists, who actually have no sense of fairness, let alone empathy, will rightly claim that so many things in the UK today are grossly unfair.

They are, of course, absolutely right.

There is justified fury at the establishment figures who have allowed our society to be broken apart for the rich. That fury is driven by real injustices and criminal acts that are treated as not worth dealing with by the establishment.

Britain is far more an unfair society than it was in 1951 when Atlee's government was defeated – and that has been deliberate government policy, particularly under Tory governments. Their arguments are basically that unfairness is necessary to encourage entrepreneurs to build the economy. We remember *greed is good* and all the other self-serving Thatcherite buzzwords. They have also espoused *trickle down economics* – and still do, even when the evidence is that far from trickle down, their economic programme is *gushing up*.

According to *The Guardian*, "The wealth of the world's 3,000 billionaires has surged by $6.5 trillion in real terms over the last decade, equivalent to 14.6% of global output. In total the richest 1% of the global population has gained at least $33.9 trillion in real terms." Keith Olsen quoting *The Guardian* on 28 June 2025, goes on to say: "The people that need money the least are the ones getting the most. Meanwhile millions are struggling just to make ends meet."

In case you are unaware of how mind-blowingly big a trillion is remember that a million seconds in elapsed time is 11 days, 13 hours and 46 minutes. A billion seconds is 31 years and 8 months. A trillion seconds is well over 31,000 years. The flow of wealth from ordinary people to a privileged and selfish miniscule minority of the world's population has been catastrophic for social cohesion, for people's lives and for the good of the world. Billionaires who have so much money they could never spend it in a lifetime dismiss the global warming catastrophe, can cheerfully cut health services for the poor and can look on at desperate people and say that they are failures because if they were successful they would be rich too.

We know that the populists, funded mostly covertly by the unimaginably rich, just lie and cheat and pretend to be on the side of ordinary people, though they are actually either billionaires or working on behalf of billionaires and multi-millionaires. Populists are controlled by rich people and are funded usually secretly by even richer people – establishment figures who've been to public and private schools – who claim to be taking on the establishment. It's a sleight of hand – fraud in other words – that is supported by the main stream media – largely owned by offshore billionaires – and populists are presented as just ordinary people taking on the entrenched ruling class, pint of beer in hand.

Nothing could be further from the truth. And they exploit grievances while offering simple solutions – *we will stop immigration, we will stop grooming gangs, we will reform the National Health Service so you can get to see your GP or have that important operation.* No matter that their solution will make it worse for ordinary people – that is all hidden. And they have a whispering campaign – *the NHS is unaffordable so we have to move to an insurance, profit-based health service; grooming gangs have been allowed to flourish because of wokery; immigrants are destroying the British way of life, the benefit system is broken and unaffordable, too many people are being diagnosed with mental health issues, there are the deserving and the undeserving poor.* When there are the real problems as outlined in this chapter, which is by no means comprehensive, the ground is set for the populists.

Wokery is pilloried by the populists because it is the opposite of what they are – it is being empathetic, understanding that diversity is a strength, and that we live in a society that needs to be good for all members of that society, young and old, no matter what race, rich and poor, able and disabled. For religious people, like Christians, it is fundamental – *love your neighbour, turn the other cheek*, and *whenever you help any one of these, you are helping me.*

People have rightly lost any trust in government. It wasn't just Johnson's lies particularly during Covid – *we followed all the* rules when the videos showed they didn't – but outright and blatant corruption, as well as what the government might call sleight of hand, but it is really deceit that has robbed successive governments of credibility and respect.

Whether it was Thatcher nearly doubling VAT in 1979 from 8% to 15% almost immediately on taking office after saying that she had no plans to increase VAT, Blair introducing student loans out of the blue with no mention in his manifesto, and then taking us into what the Iraqis rightly call *the American War*, on the basis of what is euphemistically called a *dodgy dossier* that he knew to be false, Johnson's infamous claim that we spent £350m a week with the EU and we should spend that on the NHS – with the first statement not true and the second statement an illusion – the grounds for absolute distrust of government are legion.

Take this one act of government larceny and I think fraud. All benefits, pensions and anything the government pays out are increased – when they are increased – using the *Consumer Price Index* (CPI). All areas where we pay the government, such as rail fares and student loans, are increased using the *Retail Price Index* (RPI). It is no accident but deliberate government subterfuge that for every year that CPI has been in existence it has been lower than RPI.

Why else have two measures of inflation except to trick people? It is a deliberate fraud that they hope few will notice – but everyone in their target suffers.

It is pure hypocrisy and contempt of people by successive governments, supported by the main stream media, that this isn't called out. But ordinary people know it is happening at least subliminally – and when the populists blame the Establishment for all of the abuses, you can see that it will resonate with people.

Of course the student loan fraud is made worse by the government actually charging RPI *PLUS* 3% for 35 years - meaning that it will not be paid off by the majority of ex-students ever, and becomes just another part of Pay As You Earn (PAYE).

Income tax thresholds have not kept pace with inflation since 2015. Tax allowances aren't even being increased by CPI – just another fraud on the people – dragging more and more people into standard rate tax and into higher rates of tax. And yet Starmer and Reeves can claim they haven't increased income tax – when everyone knows that as a result of what the politicians call *fiscal drag*, they are increasing the income tax take on ordinary people. This won't be changed, if Starmer and Reeves have their way, until 2029. This is just another government long term abuse.

And it makes people angry – not just the sheer arrogance that allows politicians to claim something that is just not true – but the fact that it is entirely supported by the main stream media and no-one is calling them to account. And this anger is what the populists feed upon.

And populists love austerity, as it allows them to shrink support for people and lower taxes on themselves. Austerity isn't just reducing spending on the health service, on education, on social services, and even repairing roads – but on reducing the quality of life for people. Cameron and Osborne just love the fact that they closed so many public libraries – the Tories have hated public libraries as much as they hated the NHS, as they provide benefits that the Tories don't need. As one Tory councillor said to me in all seriousness, *if people can't afford books, they shouldn't have the chance to read.* That was in the 1980s – and of course libraries provide so much more than books now, the few that remain.

Poverty is real in UK society to a scale that would have been unimaginable. We are of course talking relative poverty, that is in comparison with an average standard of living. In 2010, when the Tories and Cameron and Osborne took over, who operated as a team destroying what was left of the welfare state after Thatcher and John Major had started unravelling it, there were 3.6 million children living in relative poverty after a decade of Labour policies designed to reduce child poverty. In 2024 the figure had increased dramatically to 4.3 million children as a result of the deliberate Tory policy of hitting the poor, for example refusing to pay any benefits for more than two children in a family. Starmer has ruled out doing anything about this – why? *There is no money.* But there was plenty of money to support Israel's assault on the people of Gaza.

The squeeze on family income doesn't take into account the 33.3% increase in the rate of VAT from 15% to 20% – which disproportionately hurts people on lower incomes or on the poverty line. Of course the government claimed it was a 5% increase in VAT – lying again.

The grievances that the populists exploit are therefore real. Their solutions are, however, designed to make things worse but they never mention what those solutions are.

According to the BBC, 15 years of wage stagnation has left British workers £11,000 a year worse off – and in comparison with Germany, where we were worse off by £500 per year, it is now £4,000, partly, of course, due to Brexit. Wages have not kept up with spiralling costs and inflation so millions of ordinary people have had a vicious pay cut. The money hasn't disappeared – it has gone to the rich. If we are struggling and only just managing it is because the rich have creamed off so much – as I said, not *trickle down* but *gushing up*. This makes people quite rightly despair then get angry that even with two people in a family working they can hardly make ends meet because the rich are laughing at us and taking all the money.

Since at least 2010, the establishment or ruling class has been making life worse for ordinary people throughout the country. The NHS has been deliberately underfunded so people are forced to suffer long waiting lists and the service it provides has been silently reduced. The rich with their private health insurance are laughing. The dental service is a disgrace – not because dentists have profiteered but because their working lives and living standards have been attacked relentlessly. (That started with Thatcher of course, as did most of the ills in our country that the populists exploit, but successive governments have made it worse.)

If you are in pain or are at risk of dying because you cannot get treatment, it's not surprising that people say that things have to change and a plague on Tory and Labour politicians who parrot good words and do absolutely nothing.

The populists promise something different and of course this is attractive. The fact that they say how bad things are without actually specifying that what they are offering will make life worse is part of their con trick – similar to the one used by the Brexiters who said your life is getting worse because of the EU and it will be so much better out of the EU. As we all know, life got worse after we left the EU and it will again if the populists are allowed to succeed by Starmer and Reeves.

The promise of change is deceptively attractive as the populists have proved, as long as they don't specify how things will change. But at least that is better in some ways than Starmer and Reeves who promised change and came to power and immediately carried on the same old Tory austerity and attack on the lowest paid. Promising false change by Starmer and Reeves has just paved the way for the populists to say that the establishment will promise change but nothing will happen, whereas if you vote for us, things will certainly change and we will take on the establishment on your behalf. If you feel betrayed by Starmer and Reeves, this will have a lot of power and why wouldn't you give the populists a chance? Anything has to be better than the *same old, same old.*

And most people do feel betrayed by successive governments.

How attractive this promise of populist change can be will be seen under Trump, who promised change and is delivering the change that just under 50% of American voters apparently voted for. And the changes so passionately voted for will make the lives of the majority of people in the US worse, through tariff-induced inflation which is basically a sales tax paid by US consumers, through farm products having no market, through unemployment caused by his collapsing of the economy, through health cuts, through social security cuts, through his massive assault on the environment, through his cuts to regulations that protect people's health and livelihoods.

All central government and local government services were deliberately eroded by Cameron and Osborne who embraced *austerity* – that is taking money out of the economy – as a God-send. They could take money out of road repairs; they could reduce social services; they could cut education budgets for everyone except the 7% who were in private education; they could cut benefits for the lowest paid and force another million children into poverty (*if you can't afford to bring up children, you should have thought of that before having any)*; all the while reducing income tax for themselves and increasing indirect taxes, like VAT, which are regressive, as it means poorer people pay a higher percentage in tax than rich people as a proportion of their income.

Thatcher promised, when she started selling off council houses, that every penny raised would be ploughed back into social housing. Not a penny was spent on building new social housing and this was the start of the rise of private landlords – and so many of the old council houses are owned by private landlords charging what rent they like instead of being provided by your local council under democratic control. If your child cannot get a property to live in and some charlatan populist promises you that voting for him or her will mean you can get affordable social housing, then this is likely to make you think. That it is a lie will be defended by saying, again *the other side lie too.*

Council Tax is levied in bands A to H with a maximum. The valuation is extraordinarily based on property prices in 1991 and the maximum in band H is for properties that were valued at more than £320,001. So if your property was valued at £10 million in 1991, you would still only pay tax on £320,001. This looks unfair and it is desperately unfair, but it benefits richer people so won't change under Tories or Labour. Your council tax on your modest home may mean that you are paying the same amount of tax as the owner of a £10m estate elsewhere in the country. When the populists say that this will change under Reform – never mind they don't specify what the change will be – then this unfairness makes people angry and open to voting for the populists. With Council Tax so demonstrably unfair, why wouldn't people want something different?

National Insurance is not paid if you have a salary below £125 per month which is fair. However, if you earn £500,000 per month – and many chief executives do, and more – you pay only 2% on the amount over £4,189 per month. Everyone earning up to £4,189 per month pays 8%. How can this be fair? And the populists exploit this and say, rightly, this is rich people looking after themselves in an underhand way, while failing to acknowledge that the populists will do nothing about it. Populists don't fix things, they just exploit real issues.

Cameron and Osborne embraced with delight the economic shambles caused by the relaxation of banking regulation that they initially believed New Labour hadn't relaxed enough – having heavily criticised Blair and Brown for not taking more controls off. They then argued that Blair and Brown had been too reckless. Brazen hypocrisy.

It allowed Cameron and Osborne to pretend that taking money out of the economy would improve the economy so this gave them to excuses to, for example, increase university tuition fees to £9,000, from £3,000, and charge interest rates that would have earned amputation for usury in the Middle Ages (all with the willing support of Nick Clegg who had been successful with a manifesto that promised to abolish university tuition fees). They could take away much of the funding of local government from central funds, with the result that whereas before poorer areas were supported so that they could enjoy the same level of services as richer areas they would now be far more disadvantaged, and it meant that millionaires weren't subsidising poorer people, part of Cameron and Osborne's mission.

Starmer and Reeves have just announced in July 2025 they are relaxing the controls on the banks. There are far more important things to address and I presume this is just a deflection for us to get angry about from all the scandals and antisocial actions of the last 46 years. Won't they ever learn?

Give a banker an opportunity to create a bubble that will enrich him or her – and all of us will suffer while he or she will happily pocket the bonus and the increased salary. This act, as Chris Lewis, MP for Norwich South, has said is reckless and appalling. Improving the lives of rich bankers isn't going to help anyone and it won't produce growth – which is apparently the justification.

The Tories were able to destroy social services alongside so many other local council services, like libraries. (Educated people don't vote for populists.) They could undermine the NHS which they aren't able to abolish yet as it is still highly popular, though the populists are determined to do so, by starving it of funds. (They hoped that because of their cuts people would get so fed up with the NHS – which they always claim to be unaffordable – they could then sell it off to for-to profit driven insurance companies owned by their fellow millionaires.) They could destroy mental health support throughout the country and mental health support is at best vestigial now, with waiting lists of years. They immediately cut Sure Start, one of the most successful education programmes that New Labour brought in – because of course it largely only benefited poorer people and didn't mean anything to people sending their children to private education. They could bring in Universal Credit instead of social security, pretending it would be an improvement, although they immediately cut the rates of support.

All these cuts – whether it meant very visible things like the dreadful state of our roads now with more pot holes than ever, or virtually invisible things like destroying NHS dentistry – have provided the populists with so many grievances to exploit.

If your child has special education needs (known as SEN) – for whatever reason – there used to be a commitment to provide support to the child, the school and to the parents. Cameron and Osborne started the process of eroding the support for schools to provide SEN help – even though Cameron had a child who, in the unlikely event he went to a state school, would have probably needed SEN support. Of course that wouldn't have happened so it was easy to cut that.

If your flat is blighted by the cladding scandal that led to Grenfell burning down and you've heard the promises of Tory and Labour politicians that they will remedy this urgently and possibly reimburse you – and then nothing is done – you will be tempted by the populists promising all things to all people. And because most people not of the establishment are, as I say, fair minded, this has provided real cause for anger much wider than the up to 2 million or so affected by it. 2 million people living in fear and unable to move. How angry would you be?

The mad cow disease, bovine spongiform encephalopathy, which leads to Kreutzfelft Jacob dissease (vCJD), and the blood transfusion scandal which left 30,000 people infected and 3,000 dead was supposed to be dealt with and people treated humanely. Not a chance. Only now is there a public enquiry. This makes fair-minded people very angry. Thirty years too late.

The Post Office Horizon scandal – that blighted hundreds of lives, and seems to have been a criminal endeavour as the people in charge of the Post Office knew, or should have known (wilful blindness again) that the sub postmasters were innocent – was dreadful and people who were totally innocent – and known to be innocent or at least not known to be guilty – had their lives ruined and some sent to prison. How was it credible that 1,000 sub postmasters who had hitherto been honestly providing service to their local communities could have conspired to steal that money? Unbelievable – and no-one believes that Paul Vennels, a Church of England priest, who was CEO at the time, didn't know she was ruining people's lives without justification to protect her bonuses and position.

The Post Office, supported by successive governments, lied to the sub-postmasters – *it's not possible for the Horizon programme to be tampered with at head office; you are the only one who has been found to be fiddling the books; no-one else has complained* – and these lies – supported by Vennels – recklessly ruined people.

So many people were angered by all of this when an ITV play revealed all, that Rishi Sunak promised immediate change and compensation: immediate action. A year later? Immediate inaction. Still apparently hundreds are waiting for compensation and for an annulment of their conviction. It's apparently ok just to promise change – then do nothing. Makes me so angry – and every other fair-minded person. As of July 2025. 345 sub-postmasters, who had their lives directly and appallingly affected, have died before compensation has been paid.

The Chinook helicopter crash in 1994 is an illustration of duplicity and also the way that powerful people can avoid any retribution. In 1995 an RAF enquiry ruled that it was pilot error, in fact gross negligence. Two senior reviewing officers said this verdict was unsafe because of undisclosed serious technical issues with the Chinook and other irregularities. In 2001 an independent review cleared the crew and accepted that the RAF had falsely declared compliance with regulations. The result? Nothing. And people are rightly angry that justice was perverted and nothing was done about it. In fact the Tory Minister for Armed Forces stated that the false declaration by the RAF which led to the deaths of so many was not *wrong doing*. Of course not – that would require taking important people to court.

Thames Water (TW) is part of the privatised, monopoly water industry that Thatcher created for her chums. In the more than 40 years that it has been a private company, it has failed to invest in new reservoirs, it has failed to renew the sewers, leakages are as high as ever, pollution of our rivers and water supplies is at a disastrous level. The current Chief Executive, Chris Weston, was awarded a £195,000 bonus within 3 months of taking on the role – for no reason. (He claims that he has raised the morale of the staff – how does he know?) He also said, in a BBC documentary, that he has no idea how Thames Water ran up a debt of £20 billion. If that is true, he deserves the sack because everyone else knows that it was because Ofwat, the appalling regulator, allowed the water companies to pay out more in dividends than the profits and TW, for one, borrowed money to pay dividends and outrageous salaries and bonuses to people like Chris Weston. When someone in an apparently responsible job, being paid a significant salary and getting unearned bonuses, claims not to understand the business, it is an insult to every customer.

What is worse is that there was a revolving door between Ofwat, the incompetent if not criminal water regulator, and Thames Water – so the person in charge of Ofwat, having agreed that Thames could pay out more than the profits in dividends, then went to work at Thames Water. How convenient. And if that didn't make everyone angry, it should have done, but of course it was hidden by the gutter press.

Worse than that, the Environmental Agency has fined Thames Water hundred of millions of pounds for its pollution of our rivers and sea with raw sewage, but this means that the business is even less able to invest and will have to increase the water charges – so for the sins of the executives and shareholders, the customers have to pay twice. Why fine Thames Water thereby putting the burden and blame on the customers? Why not fine the CEO, Chris Weston – things would soon change.

People always talk about Thames Water failing – but it isn't some abstract entity, Thames Water, but highly paid and highly bonused individuals who apparently can't do the job unless they are paid extortionate amounts of money, and who then can't do the job. Chris Weston, as I have said, is the CEO and he is responsible for all the sewage going in the Thames.

South West Water (SWW) is also a case where failure is rewarded. Between 2023 and 2024 due to their lack of investment and creaming off money for shareholders and huge salaries and bonuses, pollution incidents in SWW rose 80%. The current Chief Executive Officer, Susan Davy, is leaving the company after agreeing a £24 million pay out for waste water failures. That is sewage going into the rivers or the sea. She received a pay package last year worth £803,000 for her failure and incompetence. What is particularly annoying is that sum included a £191,000 bonus for failure. She did oversee the £4.2 billion sale to Viridor - £4.2 billion for a company that has failed to invest and is now being forced to invest £20 million over 5 years instead of getting a £19 million fine. You couldn't make it up. Davy says she regrets the pollution incidents and doesn't condone them. *Condone them*? No wonder people are angry.

The regulator, Ofwat, is guilty of the complete destruction of our water industry – charged with regulating the companies, it has allowed them to avoid doing anything about future supplies (no new reservoirs have been built since 1992), water leakages were at 3 billion litres a day, has done nothing about the absurdity of the main fault in our waste water system that combines sewage and rainfall in the same system, and has bent over backwards to help the water companies defraud us all and allow huge pay increases, huge bonuses that are unearned and dividends to shareholders bigger than the profits. If you put in charge of regulation people who are likely to get a job in the water industry, you can expect nothing better. I just wonder whether any member of Ofwat can be charged with negligence or insider dealing or something more because it has failed spectacularly to regulate the water companies.

Other regulators are as bad. Ofgem, which apparently regulates the energy industry, for the benefit of the energy companies at our expense, is a shocker. It is accepted that £4 billion of excess profits were given to the energy companies by Ofgem members in 2023-2024, about £130 per household. Ofgem is refusing to return the money, although it has acknowledged its mistake, on the grounds that this will have contractual issues. Nevertheless when energy suppliers were earlier left underpaid during the energy crisis, Ofgem acted swiftly to charge all households an additional £150. Ofgem is made up of individuals and you have to wonder why they protected the energy companies and have blocked reimbursing the customers and what their hopes are about having jobs in the industry or what connections they have with energy companies. Can any members of Ofgem be sued for malpractice or charged with any offence? Clearly there is injustice here and a blatant failure to act in the interest of the customers.

It's often reported that companies have done something wrong – but that is a smokescreen. When Distillers prevaricated and acted with duplicity over the Thalidomide tragedy in the 60s and 70s, denying responsibility, pretending that there was no connection between the drug and deformity, and finally offering a pittance to children whose whole lives were blighted, it wasn't Distillers doing that, it was the Chief Executive and his board. They were the ones who should have been pilloried for their inhumane and self-seeking failure to act. They were protecting their profits, their huge salaries and their bonuses and children were being treated with callous indifference. Those individuals have to be named and shamed.

We all know that private parking operators are out of control – in fact the Tory government as far back as 2019 produced a Bill that dealt with some of the worst excesses of these sharks – for example imposing a maximum fine of £50 – instead of the £100 that they routinely charge. It also put in place a proper appeal system, as opposed to the in-house, self-serving, non-independent system run so successfully for the private parking operators. It also banned the use of aggressive language on parking tickets. Then it was withdrawn by the Tories following a legal challenge. How convenient. Apparently, according to *The Times*, 12 July 2025, the Labour Government, which is consulting about the private parking industry has decided not to do anything about the maximum and is bowing down to the private parking companies. We should be so angry about this. A hundred pounds for parking inexpertly and having a tyre over the white line! And a known scandal – with nothing being done.

Have you noticed that *Charity* is now the buzz word that the Tories use all the time. In fact the cold hand of charity was named that in the 19th century because of the abuse this caused – and it is no wonder people dislike intensely having to rely on charity. Any time soon we may find that the Charity Organisation Society, founded in 1869, is resurrected. One of its chief aims was to distinguish the *deserving poor* from the *undeserving* poor, which was a brilliant ruse to deny charitable relief to whole sections of the poor. Of course this was disguised by the rich people running it as really being focused on restoring self-sufficiency and responsibility and ensuring people didn't become dependent upon charity – but actually the main driving force was to ensure that household rates – the old system of council tax – were reduced. Tories and blue Labour love charity – it stops them having to provide money for research into cancer, into supporting disabled children and they know it is fundamentally supported by people who aren't rich themselves.

Cameron and Osborne invented the *Great Society* which was to replace as much government support for society as possible with volunteering and charity. It was also designed to take jobs away from local authorities and make them cheaper to run. Under Cameron and Osborne I used to read so many articles praising chief executives for their donations to charity – which did seem large. But of course the donations weren't large in terms of their salaries and would be much lower than the tax which should have been levied. I'm not against charity in itself, but the focus on it is entirely to benefit rich people.

Care homes and the whole care system is an absolute mess as the Tories under Johnson conceded and promised to make real changes that would mean that people were able to afford care. When it costs around £7,000 a month to provide a single room in a care home – the going rate in my area – while paying the carers the national minimum wage, you can see that care, whether in the community or in a home has to be a priority. I know that so many people are rightly upset about the failures of the care system. Johnson did absolutely nothing and Truss and Sunak did nothing too. And the Labour Government? Nothing is planned. If this doesn't make people angry, it will be because the media diverts attention towards, say, benefit cheats.

The Labour Government is using Tory arguments about the economy and reducing spending on benefits, on government employees' wages and supporting austerity which we know is self defeating. There is never the argument presented that giving poorer people more money is good for the economy as, unlike the rich recipients, they spend that money and that increases growth.

If you pay employees more, the tax take goes up and it is also possible to fund more salary increases. The arguments about Keynesian economics were all won before Thatcher and her crew, followed by nearly every government since, decided that making people poorer was good because it allowed richer people to pay them less. The Tories then exploited in-work support for workers because it meant that instead of the employer paying the staff the Government was topping up salaries. That's one reason why she said there is no such thing as society. It's curious that when it comes to dropping expensive bombs and invading countries on spurious grounds at huge expense, the money is immediately found, but when it comes to, say, restoring the pay of junior doctors to what it was in 2010, this is making the country poor and can't be afforded.

As Theresa May said in 2017, *there is no magic money tree* – except when it comes to killing people when there is always the discovery of the location of the magic money tree. It made a surprise appearance too in the Covid crisis, when the magic money tree was found for Tory donors (bribers?) who cleaned up in all the procurement for Covid-related goods to the tune of hundred of millions of pounds, a great deal of those goods were unfit for purpose and burnt. Were the beneficiaries pursued to pay back the fraudulently acquired contracts? They weren't benefit cheats and were rich and powerful and funnily enough they were left alone.

Reeves and Starmer still somehow believe that reducing spending will magically produce growth, when the last 15 years have shown that austerity drives down growth and also allows rich people to get rich by impoverishing the less well off. Why is it so important to allow bankers to have huge bonuses but drive down everyone else's standard of living? Look at what the Labour Council in Birmingham is doing to the bin workers – and how the council is supported by Reeves and Starmer. Who is more important and who is doing the most important job – a banker gambling with futures or a bin worker clearing up our rubbish?

Tax cuts are always favoured by the rich and they are said to encourage growth. The US experience is valuable and it reflects what has happened in the UK and it is the opposite. Between 1981 and 2021 tax cuts moved more than $50 trillion from the bottom 90% to the top1%. The UK experience is similar in that so many more billionaires have been created. Unions were attacked so that they have hardly any power which meant that ordinary people's salaries were driven down and the purchasing power of wages for ordinary people has been cut since 2008. Amazon's workers receive in-work state benefits because their wages are so low, while Bezos, the owner, can spend $50 million on a wedding. If this doesn't make people angry it should! And it does.

According to *The Times*, 12 July 2025, an ex-MP, Tory Craig Williams, has been charged with gambling offences relating to the date of the last general election.

His trial has been set for 2028 – I suppose to make sure that we've all forgotten about it by then. 2028! If he were a benefit claimant who had made a mistake or who had deliberately taken more benefits than they were entitled to, he'd be up before the court next week. But no – we have to protect the well-connected. I hope that makes you as angry as it makes me.

When the bankers collapsed our economy in 2008 by pure greed, the banks were rescued by the government at huge cost – at our cost. Instead of, say, giving every family in the country £10,000 to keep the economy afloat, the government gave the equivalent amount to bankers who continued to enjoy their vastly inflated salaries even though they had caused the problem in the first place. No matter that, as I have said, they were aided by Blair's government which had reduced regulation (and the Tories claimed then that New Labour hadn't gone far enough in giving bankers free rein to destroy our livelihoods). And Starmer and Reeves are proposing to reduce regulations on bankers again.

Companies like Apple, Google, Amazon and Starbucks have a brilliant way of avoiding tax. They headquarter themselves in Ireland – where corporation tax is extremely low – and all their transactions are apparently in Ireland for tax purposes. The profits they make on UK sales and purchases are effectively laundered through Ireland. Google, for instance paid £36 million in tax on £1,000,000,000 of revenue in 2017. The claim is that Google is an international company and not a UK company therefore most of its profits here don't count. The other companies do the same. Then HMRC did a sweetheart deal with Google that increased the tax paid but nothing like the tax it should be on the profits made in the UK. This is just so unfair – and we should not have to put up with it. But where are Starmer and Reeves? Cutting benefits of disabled people.

It has just been revealed that HMRC has no idea about how many billionaires there are in this country and who they are. It focuses on ordinary people as they can't fight back – but ignores billionaires. Parliament's spending watchdog has said that this represents *significant opportunities to collect more revenue* – but as it is the rich, and they are probably donors, nothing happens.

Another totally insidious and appalling, and little known, abuse of our country is contained in trade deals – the Investor-State Dispute Settlement. This is a secret weapon of, say, the oil industry. It allows corporations to sue countries in secretive *corporate courts* – the UK is one they can sue – when government implement policies corporations find restrictive of their ability to help destroy the zero-carbon initiative or when they aim to dodge corporation tax. When political parties are in thrall to large corporations it is inevitable that these abuses will be brought in – deliberately secretly and deliberately against the public interest.

We also need to look at our two tier so-called justice system. You will know that anyone defrauding benefits is rightly punished. On the other hand, bankers behaving appallingly and supporting drug cartels are not even charged. The story of HSBC and the drugs cartels is one that will illustrate this perfectly.

In 2021, HSBC was fined £63.9m for failings in its money laundering controls. But this wasn't the first fine – nor the first offence – and was a fine for criminal failings over an 8 year period from 2010-2018. HSBC did not dispute the findings – and in fact got a 30% reduction in the fine for agreeing to pay the fine. (Try that on a magistrates' court judgment!) HSBC received numerous warnings during the period 2010-2018 and largely was able to ignore them.

In 2012, before that scandal, HSBC was hit with a fine of $1.9 billion, coupled with $665 million in civil penalties, for most notably serving as a conduit for Mexican drug cartels. Notice it is the bank that is fined – none of the directors and non-executive directors received a fine, but those directors earned enormous salaries and bonuses on the back of the increased profits HSBC made. Not a single director was arrested let alone charged for providing such personally profitable services to drug cartels. In 2012 HSBC and its directors were allowed to get away with this and to keep their banking licence. Apparently the regulators let this happen as they didn't want a prominent financial institution to collapse. How convenient and how one-sided. So if you are a small time drug dealer – you go to jail when caught. If you are a banker knowingly providing financial services to drug cartels – both Columbian and Mexican – you get away with no penalty and you can carry on doing business. How convenient.

This however wasn't the start of the drug trafficking that was facilitated by HSBC executives and directors. In the early 2000s, HSBC's executives and directors knowingly – or they should have known – laundered

$881million for the drug cartels. This wasn't an oversight – but systematic failures.

In addition, in the 2012 settlement, HSBC admitted violating US sanctions against Iran and it had, for years, circumvented the sanctions in various ways.

So bankers were clearly guilty of supporting and enabling the most horrible crimes from which they benefited. How many went to jail? How many were charged? How many were even arrested? You're right – none. They were too rich and powerful to have to face justice. (For a really full account do look at *Dirty Money* which is a Netflix programme about how HSBC kept promising to clean things up and kept falling foul of the law and regulations because it did nothing.) HSBC executives were effectively drug dealers – but if you are rich and powerful, you can get away with it. Let us be clear, it wasn't actually HSBC – it was the directors and executives who were the people who did this. How do they live with themselves?

It wasn't just HSBC executives and directors of course, other banks shared in the bonanza – but it was apparently the most egregious. So if you ever doubt that the rich and powerful are protected from receiving justice, you can investigate this further. As *Investopedia* commented: *the source of these failures* [sic] *was a corporate culture that prioritized profits over ethical conduct.* You have to wonder how many victims of HSBC's executives there are whose lives were blighted by the drugs trade. We have a right to be so angry that not one of the executives was even arrested.

Of course, as with so many things, the regulator was at fault too. For years the US Office of the Comptroller of Currency (OCC) had apparently been aware of HSBC's anti-money laundering deficiencies but had failed to take decisive action. It was the Securities and Exchange Commission that fined HSBC and there are strong links between the US regulators and the UK's regulators, essentially the Financial Conduct Authority (FCA). The FCA – or its predecessor – will have known exactly what HSBC was up to and presumably knew about the fines and the reason for the fines but it also didn't institute any criminal proceedings against the executives lining their pockets with drug dealing.

The interest rate rigging prosecutions which resulted in what the Supreme court calls *unsafe conviction* of the traders who were given quite extraordinary sentences has been exposed by the BBC which has said that the real culprit was the Bank of England. Naturally there will be no charges of senior Bank of England people who, the BBC say, manipulated interest rates to ensure that Barclay's Bank didn't have to be nationalised. Once again important people are protected.

Then there are the sweetheart deals between the UK's His Majesty's Revenue and Customs (HMRC) and various corporates over the failure to pay corporation tax. Vodaphone, for example, had an £84 billion tax avoidance bonanza. That was *avoidance* which is legal if not ethical – while executives shared £500 million in fees from the take over of Verizon. Later however HMRC agreed a deal to let Vodaphone off a £6 billion tax bill. Contrast that with the case of people who don't earn enough to pay tax in the UK who are required to fill in a tax return – which can be reasonable – but if they don't, they get fined – and one woman at least has been fined £10,000 and others driven into bankruptcy when they were probably not aware of what was going on and were overtaken by events. Some time ago the Tory government recognised the issue and said the maximum fine should be no more than £200 – and, as usual, then did nothing about it. Vodaphone let off £6 billion- people in difficulties who might not understand the system fined £10,000.

This is a two tier system again – and if you are rich and powerful, you are protected. Ordinary people are treated to the full force of the law and despite soothing words when the injustice is publicised, nothing is done.

Stamp Duty on house purchase is basically corrupt as foreign companies and individuals don't apparently need to pay it. It's also a brilliant example of *fiscal drag* – because fifty years ago people buying the average priced house would pay very little but as house prices have increased – partly because foreign nationals, not immigrants as these are rich people and therefore don't count as immigrants, have been buying up our houses without having to pay stamp duty – the point at which stamp duty is payable has not kept pace with inflation. It is another governmental sleight of hand. Stamp duty is now a considerable burden and a real bar to some people buying a house and getting on the housing ladder.

Capital Gains Tax – the amount paid on the profit if you sold something, for examples shares – is taxed at different rates. For higher tax rate payers it is 24% if you sell residential property other than your main residence,

32% on gains from *carried interest* and 24% on other chargeable assets. For a basic rate tax payer, the rate is 18% for gains on residential property, but not your own home, 32% on gains from *carried interest*, and 18% from gains on other chargeable assets. (*Carried Interest* is a special wheeze for fund managers and is focused on the share of profits a fund manager gets as a performance fee.) Why aren't capital gains treated as ordinary income and subject to the 20%, 40% and 45% tax bands that ordinary people pay rather than this special treatment for people who produce nothing other than money?

Rail privatisation was and is an absolute scandal – and much of the scandal was hidden by the apparently corrupt Department for Transport. The way the bidding worked for the new franchises was a real scandal. Basically the bidding companies had to promise a return to the state for running the railways in their franchise. Franchises were awarded on how much return the companies promised. All well and good you might think, except that the bidding companies came up with bidding strategies that were accepted by the government at face value but were fraudulent. Essentially they took on, say, a seven year franchise. For the first two or three years they demanded subsidies *as they got their business in order*, and then promised fabulous returns in years four, five, six and seven. At the end of three years they handed back the franchise with no penalty, having taken all the subsidies, reduced the service and made a rather good profit.

The private rail companies have a propaganda public statement which says that their profits are only 3% of the revenue. What they don't say is that the executives cream off huge salaries and bonuses. David Brown running Govia in the 2010s, had a salary before bonuses of more than £2 million. He also discovered that not employing enough drivers and therefore having to cut services resulted in fines, but the fines were less than the cost of employing the right number of staff. So services were cut.

David Brown had another wheeze, totally supported by Philip Rutnam, then Permanent Secretary at the Department for Transport (DfT), and disguised by the DfT, denied by it, and subject to the utmost deflection and deception, fully supported by the Head of the Civil Service and Cabinet Secretary, Jeremy Heywood, (who worked at one time at the same American bank as Rutnam), the Chief Executive of the Civil Service, John Manzoni, and the Director General of Ethics and Propriety, Susan Grey, who used wilful blindness writing that she had seen no evidence to support my case – to ensure Rutnam was exonerated. The scam was focused on the so-called *Independent Penalty Fares Appeals Service* (IPFAS).

By law, IPFAS had to be separate from the railway companies. It assessed appeals against the penalty fares imposed by train companies. It took me two years to find out that IPFAS was neither independent nor separate, but run as a profit making department inside Govia, the train operating company whose CEO is David Brown. So Govia reviewed appeals against Govia imposed penalty fares, threatened anyone who appealed with criminal court if they didn't pay up and contributed to Govia's profits.

The DfT knew all of this, denied it to my face on several occasions, and when I complained to Jeremy Heywood about the scandal, Rutnam authorised the statement that *IPFAS was run as an arms-length subsidiary of Govia.* (As if that meant it wasn't run by a train operating company!) Heywood accepted this despite the fact that there is no such thing as *an arms-length subsidiary* and, as you have seen, IPFAS was just another department inside Govia. To get this information, blanked out in a Freedom of Information (FoI) response, I had to go to the Lower Tribunal, where I was up against two barristers and a tribunal chairman who thought the DfT would be justified in withholding information as otherwise it might *chill* civil servants from doing their job and senior civil servants shouldn't be subject to scrutiny, then to the Higher Tribunal where a High Court judge agreed with me that senior civil servants should be even more subject to FoI requests, and such blatant acts by the DfT and Cabinet Office should be exposed.

No sanctions were applied to Rutnam (awarded £300,000 damages for being mistreated by Priti Patel), to Jeremy Heywood, Susan Gray or John Manzoni. Wilful blindness pays. In addition, no appeals to IPFAS were reviewed and it was allowed to carry on making money for David Brown and Govia. I was told that it would be too expensive to review all the appeals, so I said that we should avoid that expense and Govia should just pay back every fine that had been appealed against.

You might not be surprised that I imagined that there was some cosy relationship between Rutnam and Brown – who had run public transport in London at a much lower salary when it was nationalised – and this was confirmed to me by a junior civil servant who said that nothing would ever be done about Govia's tricks. And nothing was.

Heywood by the way left the Civil Service is 2004 under a cloud – Google it – went to work for that American bank, and the when the fuss died down came back at the most senior level in the Civil Service.

Rail fares have increased since privatisation by more than 21% in real terms, mainly to pay the private companies' shareholders and the excessive salaries of the executives.. The Rail Delivery Group, the body that protects the interest of the shareholders, says that 98p or 97p in the pound goes to running services – but *running services* in their definition is not mine. They never disclose what they include as *running* services and it apparently includes the huge bonuses that the executives enjoy at our expense. The objective of privatisation was to stop the government subsidising the railways so much. The fares now deter people from using trains.

The position of WASPI – *Women Against State Pension Inequality*- is fascinating. Having accepted that there had been maladministration, because women were not fully informed about the rise in the state pension age from 60 to 66, successive governments had firmly refused to pay compensation. This was appalling. For once the Parliamentary and Health Service Ombudsman forced the issue and the women are to receive £2,950 as compensation. It shows that the tireless pressure that the women brought can work – and we need to ensure that other campaigns are similarly rewarded. It will apparently cost £10 billion – and of course won't be an automatic payout – women have to claim it. There is a view that this sum doesn't match the losses – so further action is planned. Why does it take relentless campaigning to get what has already been conceded is right?

Reeves' budget was disastrous as the rise in unemployment has shown – although we knew that. Increasing National Insurance rates for employers looks a good political move as it is almost a stealth tax which the general public may not notice or understand– but in fact increasing employers' costs is always going to affect the ability to employ people. It just shows how much Reeves is in thrall to the rich donors to the Labour Party that she will do almost anything to avoid a wealth tax.

Our country is currently being carved up by hedge funds and vulture capitalists, supported by both Tory and Labour politicians to create so-called *Special Economic Zones* (SEZs) and Freeports where new rules can be invented by the owners of these SEZs, where existing environmental protection and existing regulations can be forgotten, where democratic government becomes irrelevant and where the rich can carve up property and money for their own benefit. We have already seen examples of corruption that haven't been dealt with. The hedge funds and vulture capitalists will be able to ignore labour regulations, safety regulations and probably most tax. The idea is to attract Foreign Direct Investment (FDI) but why the foreign direct investors shouldn't obey our laws is another establishment wheeze. I don't think people are angry about this yet – but they should be and when we make this public knowledge with our campaign, they will be.

According to *Private* Eye, the position of the Teeside SEZ and freeport is dire and at the heart of the issue is NE Security Ltd, which is tasked with monitoring goods entering this zone. This is a highly responsible role as the well-documented history of freeports has shown that they are easily exploited for illicit activities, such as money laundering, drug trafficking and smuggling. The majority owner of NE Security Ltd is David Garside Snr, currently involved in a dispute over a £1.5m tax bill, having dissolved a previous company to evade creditors. In *Private Eye* 1633, it is stated that the managing director of the company is David Garside Jnr, who is serving a lengthy prison sentence for his role in a cocaine-running operation. It seems like a licence to evade the law while masquerading as a legitimate security operation. The Labour Government is doing absolutely nothing about this – which, in effect is to say that Starmer and Reeves have endorsed it.

We have seen how the populists work in their Brexit campaign, built on lies and deception. The Brexiters now justify their lies by saying that the Remain campaign lied too! That is they don't deny their campaign was based on lies. What they exploited was the fact that so many people's lives had been blighted by Cameron and Osborne, wages were lower than in 2008, the NHS was struggling, councils couldn't provide basic services like weekly bin collections, and the populists were able to blame all of this on the EU, state that the EU was an establishment stitch up, and that change would be good as we would have our sovereignty back. What it meant was that the value of the pound sank, manufacturing plants closed, and our freedoms were compromised and freedom of movement was stopped. Deflection, wilful blindness and hypocrisy – with the arch liar, Johnson, able to brush it all off with the support of the billionaire-owned press. And hardly coincidentally the incoming EU law on tax transparency that would have exposed the dodgy dealings of so many of the rich backers of the populists was not brought in. Funny that.

The way that offshore billionaires and millionaires funnel money to right wing extreme political parties is very clever. Although it is apparently against the law for a foreigner to donate to a political party, they set up shell companies in the UK and channel the money through that. But this is not the most important and secretive route. There are shadowy groups called *unincorporated associations*. These bodies don't need to have a formal structure, file accounts or even reveal where their money comes from. Crucially it is perfectly legal for foreign money from AfD linked billionaires and others to be funnelled to these right wing extreme parties. More than £60 million of unrevealed money has been channelled into them so far. How can this be legal? Even David Blunkett is on record as saying that this is dangerous and distorts our political dialogue. Most people will be angry about this when it is revealed how the populists are funded by people who have absolutely no interest in the well-being of our people.

Mainstream media, although less important today, and social media are a malign influence on our society – with GB News claiming it does not have to support opposing opinions because, despite its name it is an entertainment station and not a news station. It is pure propaganda and we need to ensure that it and social media are subject to what the US used to have – a *Fairness Doctrine* – abolished by Reagan. The anonymity of social media, the lawlessness of the mainstream media should make people angry.

So what the populists do is find or expose real grievances, claim that they will make such changes that will improve life – without specifying that those changes are – and then use the press and broadcasting to claim that they are on the side of the little people. Those grievances are real – the populists' solutions are merely exploitative and fraudulent – but saying that only makes their case. The populists say all establishment politicians are the same – so if we accuse them of lying, then they say it proves their point.

Reform wants to make £80 billion of unfunded tax cuts. Nigel Farage's economic policy is identical to Liz Truss's - which crashed the economy and sent mortgages spiralling.

I've said that the populists are very careful not to spell out what they will actually do, Nevertheless, we can see some of their attitudes and policies. Farage for instance isn't on the side of working people. He voted against the Employment Rights Bill, which will end fire-and-rehire and extend parental rights. We know whose side he is really on?

He announced he would give a tax cut to foreign millionaires. Man of the people? Not only would this be a golden giveaway to the rich, but experts warn this would leave a massive hole in the country's finances, that we'll be left to pick up the bill for.

He'd make families worse off. He voted against making school uniforms cheaper, and free breakfasts for primary school children. Says it all.

As a member of the European Parliament, he was disruptive and also largely absent. His record now as MP for Clacton – an area with good reason to be angry with Conservative and Labour governments – is patchy – turning up more often in the US – for example at Trump's inauguration.

If this list of scandals and corruption and the failures of our society and justice system to do anything about it makes you as angry as I am, you can see that it provides an absolute golden opportunity for the populists like Farage. Chapter 2 looks at what we can do about this and prevent the populists from exploiting the horrible state of our country after 46 years of rich people enriching themselves.

We have had enough of words – now we need action and if Starmer and Reeves aren't the people to do it, then they should be replaced. Otherwise we are giving the country to the populists and that will mean the end of so many of the areas of our life that are important. Labour MPs in marginal seats know that the policies of Starmer and Reeves are making their position worse – so they have to act.

Chapter 2

The Manifesto to Create Hope, Trust and Unity

There is a real appetite for change in the country partly caused by all the corruption of the 14 years of Tory government but mainly because of all the absolutely valid causes of anger and fury that are outlined in Chapter 1. Populists play into this anger and deflect it onto minorities using the old *Daily Mail* and fascist nasty tactic of *them* and *us*. The media then exaggerate everything that makes any particular minority look bad – favourite is migrants, but it also includes, for example, Muslims (it was the Jews in the 1930s for the *Daily Mail*), Asians, trans people, homosexuals, blacks, climate change activists, demonstrators, any workers asking for a pay increase and people who support Palestine.

It is an uncomfortable fact for the media and the establishment that Jeremy Corbyn's Labour Party fought the 2017 general election on a progressive and demonstrably fair manifesto, offering hope, and won 12.9 million votes, and this despite the sabotaging insiders in the Labour Party, like Stephen Kinnock, who did everything they could to undermine the campaign and Jeremy Corbyn. Kinnock's face, shown on national television, when he heard the news of Corbyn's near success told the whole story – he was so upset and disappointed. He preferred to keep the Tories. How disgraceful.

Corbyn nearly won and Theresa May only received 13.67 million votes and had to rely on the DUP of Northern Ireland. On the other hand, Keir Starmer won an overwhelming 166 seat majority on 9.7 million votes – 3.2 million votes less than Corbyn managed in 2017. Corbyn was vilified as an antisemite, the BBC presented him as a stooge for Russia, and he still nearly succeeded with progressive policies. In 2019 when Corbyn failed spectacularly it was partly because he refused to oppose Brexit, while the media had had a field day supporting Liar Johnson – and not exposing any of the underhand tricks the Tories were using.

So there is an appetite now for change – and for progressive policies of the type Corbyn espoused – and it is with those progressive policies and all the remedies for the scandals and corruption of the last 45 years that we can outflank the populists despite the support of Murdoch, Jonathan Harmsworth, and other offshore billionaires who secretly fund the populists. We have to create a narrative of hope and possibilities for ordinary people but first we have to have action that addresses the scandals, gets redress, charges bankers for supporting drugs cartels and shows ordinary people that there can be real change – and a better, united society.

We know there will be a blizzard of attacks on MPs and campaigners who stand up to these ruthless offshore billionaires, but like Corbyn in 2017, they can break through.

We have to redirect people's anger onto the people who caused this mess – and abolish the concept of austerity, self-defeating and only a weapon in the Tories' class war – and make a difference as quickly as possible to people's lives.

Our biggest weapon outflanking the populists is actual action. We know where the magic money tree is now – let's use it.

I acknowledge we can't address all the issues immediately but we have to have a plan that addresses all the things that make people angry and show them that we are doing something about the most important. It will be as usual priorities but immediate action is still possible.

Before starting on what is to be done, which will inevitably mean changing many taxes, increasing investment in infrastructure and people, we will apparently be open to the attack that it is fiscally irresponsible. There are a number of points that need to be made in support of our approach – plus the fact that we propose immediately increasing some taxes.

There are a series of statements that are apparently accepted by Labour, the Tories and Reform which are bogus – and not just if you believe, as I do, in *New Monetary Theory* and Keynesian economics, which we know works for ordinary people.

Most of these false statements started with Thatcher, such as government finances are like a family's finances. This is completely untrue. Families, for a start, can't just print money – as the Labour Government and successive Tory Governments did following the 2008 financial crash, in order to support the reckless bankers who had caused the crash.

If anyone doubts that money can be found when it is needed, just think of the way that when defence needs money, it's found immediately. How much has been spent by Starmer on supporting Israel's assault on the people of Gaza? Less contentiously, money was found during the Covid crisis to keep people employed as well as rewarding Tory donors with hugely profitable contracts.

Yes, defence is important and more important with every action Trump takes, but so too is ensuring that children don't live in poverty because a life blighted at an early age is a life ruined forever in so many cases. Buying new submarines and planes and bombs is always possible but somehow keeping 4 million children in poverty is solely because you don't have any money. Not caring for the mentally ill is justified because we have no money.

Find another Iraq and the money will be found immediately. It's almost a case of having to say *really?* whenever the tired hacks and politicians claim that there is no money. First the government must abolish its two child limit for benefits and do this quickly – this will make an extraordinary difference and remove a stain on our society.

As we have seen, there is a view that taking money out of the economy is good for the economy – so austerity is justified. Actually Keynes was proved right – look what Roosevelt did in the 1930s by building roads and dams and bridges and investing in people. The economy which had been driven into the ground by austerity and tariffs was revived without worrying too much about the national debt because it would be reduced in time by growth, and as a result unemployment was reduced and people could stand tall again. The amount gained in taxes more than repaid the investment in people and projects.

If a person is made unemployed, immediately the tax take is reduced. It never makes sense even when the people who point out that inflation will go up if we keep people employed or raise their wages, hog the stage. If most inflation is caused by price hikes out of the control of people in this country, for example when oil prices rise, what sense does it make to increase our interest rates – the favoured way of defeating inflation? Immediately people lose jobs and the tax take goes down.

As wages have been deliberately kept low and below the rate of inflation for 15 years, we need immediate action by the government to ensure that wages are increased to what they would have been in 2025 allowing for inflation since 2008. If this has to be paid out of the salaries of the Chief Executive and the other executives, so much the better. For too long they have milked the system. The argument that you have to bribe these people with excessive salaries and bonuses is bogus and they need to be part of this society, not merely profiting from it.

All NHS staff should have their salaries restored to what they were in 2010 allowing for inflation measured by RPI. This isn't a zero sum game as the tax that they will pay will be much higher too. This will show commitment to ordinary people – but people who are also highly gifted and highly valued and so important to every one of us.

The creeping privatisation of the NHS and the covert way that the services it provides have been cut back also needs immediate attention – and a commitment to bringing the NHS back to what it provided

Dentists should also have their terms and conditions and their salaries looked at so we can once again have a flourishing NHS dentistry – where people can afford to look after their teeth. Thatcher, of course, increased dental charges enormously – it didn't particularly bother her with her wealth – and successive governments have built on that while discouraging dentists to work in the NHS. Let's move back to the old system which worked very well until Thatcher got her hands on it,

Making ordinary people poorer through interest rate increases doesn't help them nor does it help the economy. It also doesn't reduce the national debt and it increases the gap between what the government spends and what it receives in tax because it means that the government has to pay more interest on its debts.

But we are going to reduce inflation at a stroke without hurting ordinary people – indeed by the specific means that helps ordinary people most and which the Tories used to increase the misery of ordinary people.

VAT must be reduced, first by 25% to 15% from its current 20%. It is an indirect tax and hurts lower paid people who inevitably pay a higher percentage of their money in tax than richer people. That is totally unfair.

Remember that in 1979, Thatcher knew that to break the unions she would have to increase unemployment – eventually to over 3 million, even after she had fiddled the definition of what it meant to be unemployed. She was determined to make people she was going to make unemployed still pay tax. VAT was increased overnight to nearly double – from 8% to 15%. Subsequently the Tories increased it to 17.5% and then to 20%. We ought to aim to get VAT back to 8%, but let's immediately make the rate 15% and see how that goes.

Inflation will be reduced at a stroke. It is probable (if you believe all the right wing think tanks that reducing taxation stimulates the economy and makes the tax take higher) that the economy will boom, there will be the growth in GDP that Starmer and Reeves are so focused on and more people will be able to buy more things and everyone will be happy.

This will be extremely popular – even with rich people paying VAT on school fees.

The only argument against is that people on benefits will pay less tax. Great.

This is a concrete, demonstrable action to help people and will make a difference showing people that the government does understand.

We must have a wealth tax on all people with assets over £10 million. At the very least this will pay for the lowering of the VAT rate.

We must abolish means tested benefits. Before Cameron and Osborne every family with children in education, received Family Benefit. When it was Child Allowance, before the Tories got their hands on it, it wasn't means tested, but it had to be declared for tax purposes and was taxed as part of one's income. This is so much cheaper to administer using an existing reasonably efficient method of ensuring that the benefit only went to people who needed it whereas checking that people are not entitled to it is costly and self-defeating. It does have the benefit to the government that some people who are entitled to it won't claim it – but this is unfair and a sleight of hand unworthy of government. There were all those Tories saying that the money was going to people who didn't need it – but taxing it will ensure that it does go to the people who need it and not to the rich.

Cameron and Osborne, of course, made it both complex and unfair. If one parent in a family earned over £50,000 no Family Allowance was paid. But if two parents in a family both earned under £50,000 then Family Allowance was paid. So two people earning £99,998 could get Family Allowance but a one parent family where the parent earned £51,000 received none. And people had to work out if and when they would cross the threshold and ensure that they told the government not to pay them. Ridiculous, expensive, open to all sorts of manipulation, difficult to administer – grossly unfair. Typical Tory logic.

The same applies to all other taxable benefits which should not be means tested. Tax them through Pay As You Earn (PAYE), income tax, if they get more money than their personal allowance.

As we said in Chapter 1, Council Tax is completely unfair. We will abolish the current bands, do a revaluation of property prices, perhaps using Zoopla, and charge a tiny percentage of the value of the house as Council Tax. At the same time, we will restore the funding for local government that Cameron and

Osborne took away because they didn't want people living in a poorer area to pay less, and, in fact, by and large and deliberately by Cameron and Osborne design, households in poorer areas pay higher Council Tax than households in richer areas and certainly a higher percentage of their income.

We will restore the amount of money that councils receive from central government – so that the levelling up that was part of the social contract before Cameron and Osborne destroyed it will actually be achieved, rather than being a slogan that had no actual meaning. This must happen immediately so people can see their council tax reduced.

Apparently Starmer has agreed that funding of political parties through shell companies laundering offshore billionaires' money to extreme right wing organisations, and other parties as well, will become a criminal offence, but they need to go further and ensure that unincorporated associations are also banned. This is urgent and highly significant for all of the health of our democracy.

The water companies that the Tories created as monopolies – while pretending that competition and private industry would provide a better service – must be nationalised and the debts that they have run up – over £20 billion in Thames Water's case – be paid back by the shareholders. There are provisions that exist to keep the taps flowing and the sewage dealt with, and the best is hiving off all the assets to a separate new company, and leaving the debt with the shareholders of Thames Water. That way the people who have profited over the years by destroying the water company and taking dividends more than the profits and failing to invest, will have to pay the price of their greed and failure. The new company should not include the executives who currently run the company and who have just displayed a total failure to be responsible with our money.

In the fifty or so years under private rapacity, the water companies were allowed to pay out in dividends and salaries for the top executives, more than their profits – and they did so, failing to renew the sewers, build reservoirs and make the structural changes needed to an outdated Victorian system. There was no control but an apparently corrupt water regulator – Ofwat – that looked after the interests of the directors, hedge funds and shareholders and forgot about the consumers paying the bills.

The Environment Agency (EA) has fined water companies for fouling the environment – though of course the Tories reduced the monitoring of the environmental impact of sewage flowing into our rivers and seas so there would be fewer headlines. But fining, say, Thames Water is really fining the customers because it takes money out of the company which the customers have to make up. If instead of fining us, if the EA had fined the CEO and the other directors of Thames Water for their illegal disregard of environmental standards, things would have changed pretty quickly. But no – EA had to look after the shareholders and directors..

Prior to nationalisation, Ofwat needs to be abolished and reconstituted with elected members whose primary interest will be security of supply, cleanliness of our rivers and seas, and service to customers, while also insisting that the current system of foul water being in the same sewers as rain water is abolished and ensure that two separate systems will sit side by side. At the same time, the Consumer Council for Water (CCW) can safely be abolished as it never does any good – in my experience all it ever tried to do was fob me off and close my complaint as soon as possible before it upset Thames Water. It is also powerless as far as I understand, without the clout to force the water companies to comply with the law. When our sewer overflows from being blocked, the sewage goes straight in the Thames. CCW fobbed me off about that.

Belatedly the government has now decided to abolish Ofwat and replace it with a regulator with more powers. But it will be stuffed with the usual apologists for the water companies who will go out of their way to avoid any sanctions on the executives of the water companies..

And those lackeys and lobbyists, usually employed in some way by the water companies who claim that nationalisation will be more expensive than leaving the privatised companies alone, have prepared the most dubious figures to support their case. There is no doubt that paying private industry salaries and bonuses and dividends is much more expensive than a nationalised service with proper long term planning. We can use capitalists' tricks to leave the debt with TW and create a new water company, for instance.

We must also abolish the other current regulators such as Ofgem which have completely ignored the needs of customers and given the companies they are supposed to control freedom to do what they like. They too must be reconstituted with elected members to control the various industries they are supposed to be concerned with.

The private parking companies must be brought to heel. The legislation is there – we don't need another enquiry or consultation as Starmer and Reeves are insisting on – it just needs to be implemented and that can happen easily within days. That weapon of government – a further enquiry to push legislation down the road, is a gross distortion of what needs to be done.

Straightaway the government must stop having two measures of inflation – CPI, which is nearly always a lower measure and RPI, the higher measure – and manipulating it so we pay the government at the higher rate and the government pays out at the lower rate. It is just basically fraud. CPI should be abolished as it doesn't take into account housing costs.

Student loans should be abolished. They tax people for wanting to better themselves when we actually will need more highly trained people to work in the AI economy, but worse than that, they create a permanent debt for over 35 years at usurious rates of interest. Originally when Blair introduced them – without having mentioned what he was planning to do in the Labour Party manifesto – the fees were £3,000 per year and the interest rate was highly subsidised. The Tories, supported by Clegg's LibDems (who had promised to abolish them in their manifesto) tripled the fees to £9,000 (and now to £9,250), and imposed an interest rate of RPI (note the higher rate of inflation) PLUS 3%. Whereas under Blair it was confidently predicted that most people would pay off their loan within the then 30 year limit, now only a minority will pay it off within the 35 years the Tories made it. Of course this didn't affect rich people as they paid off their offsprings' debt immediately and so only less well off people had to pay this inordinate tax. And for those who currently have student debt, we must reduce the interest rate to the Bank of England interest rate as a first step towards cancelling the debt.

We need a more highly educated population not a dumbed down one – and despite the pious statements that poorer people are not put off by the thought of paying an extra 9% income tax for most of their working life, we know this is absolutely false. Tinkering with this outrageously unfair tax on graduates is not enough – and student loans and the expensive paraphernalia that surrounds it – including the Student Loans Company – should be immediately abolished. This will be highly popular.

Wes Streeting has proposed writing off at least part of the doctors' student loan debt as part of his settlement of the dispute over their pay. This proves that it can be done – and it should be done now.

One of the calculated effects of this new regime, is that the arts and humanities are being squeezed out of our national life – as university after university drops the courses. So the Gradgrinds and the Goves destroy a valuable aspect of our national life – despite the fact that it is important too as it earns valuable foreign exchange.

I have no objection to chief executives and other directors earning good money, but they should be limited to a salary, including bonuses, of no more than 40 times their lowest paid worker as in the 1960s. If they claim that they need bribing to do their job, and £200,000 per week, I don't think they are being honest with themselves. Of course, they could increase the salary of the lowest paid and that would help them. Instead we have remuneration committees – apparently completely objective because they are made up at least in part of non-executive directors – that decide executives' salaries and they always claim that they have to pay £5 million a year to CEOs to attract them to the job. But hang on a minute, those apparently objective non-executive directors usually come from other companies and they scratch the back of the executives in the company they are working on as independent directors, and expect that the directors they have rewarded will do the same for them. Totally fixed and largely corrupt.

The threshold for Stamp Duty must be index linked to what it was in 1970 for the average house.

Cameron and Osborne did do one thing that was sensible (as though they were concerned with fairness!) – in the past once you reached a threshold, you paid Stamp Duty on the whole purchase price. Cameron and Osborne made it that you paid it only on the amounts above the thresholds. They also introduced higher rates for higher priced houses – and, for once, that seems fair.

One of Cameron and Osborne's most cynical approaches was to cut the justice system. You might think that the Tory Party which regards itself as the law and order party would ensure that the justice system is robust. But the danger to them was that knowing what they wanted to do, they might get trapped by the law, so they defunded it to the point where getting justice is nearly impossible. There are now 400,000 cases – 320,00 in the magistrates court and 80,00,00 in the crown court – that are waiting to be heard. If you believe as I do that justice delayed is justice denied this is an outrage. We must restore funding to the justice system to what it was in 2010 adjusted for inflation – so that no longer is it a year between charging a rapist and him appearing in court. This is unfair to the victims, unfair to the accused – and a denial of justice to the victims and the accused. This isn't a government commitment that can be just words. We need to see it in action.

The state of our prisons is also scandalous – again the party that pretends it is the party of law and order reduced the prison service to a shadow of itself, and the stories of drones delivering drugs, of inadequate supervision, no rehabilitation and a break down in staff morale mean that governments have failed. We need a total commitment to improving our prisons – and immediate action.

Capital Gains Tax will be payable as though it is income and will be subject to the income tax bands and the tax will be paid through the normal system. Reeves can do this immediately.

The income tax thresholds should be immediately increased and index linked back to 2015 when they were frozen by the Tories.

National Insurance – which we must keep separate in the sense of being ring-fenced – should perhaps be part of income tax or we could just ensure that National

Insurance is paid on the full amount of earnings at the standard rate. If we want to raise the same amount of money from National Insurance, this will allow us to lower the rate of National Insurance for everyone other than the very rich.

Starmer, Reeves and Angela Raynor must act fast to stop the proliferation of SEZs and freeports – we already know that they are highly suspicious – and immediate action is required to abolish them. It was of course a Tory fiddle – and every day that goes by with Starmer and Reeves doing nothing is an insult to honest people and an attack on our democracy. Angela Raynor has apparently said, again according to *Private Eye* that there is no need for a review – and she must be disabused of this and understand that people are rightly outraged.

Charities have a role to play in our social life, but they should not be a substitute for proper social care, proper mental health support and proper medical research. We should examine again what is right for charities to do – supplementing rather than being the main source – and look carefully at taking back into the NHS and the care system what should be our responsibility as a society.

There is no time to waste in developing and implementing a proper care system in this country – we are a rich country and we must be able to look after our elderly and those who are too ill or disabled to look after themselves. It is a disgrace that Johnson could promise a comprehensive care system then do absolutely nothing – like his promise to build 40 new hospitals. We know he was just making things up and lying – and now the government has to act and show that they care. No more empty words. There can be an immediate commitment to making a national care service.

Schools have been running on air for the last 10 years at least – and we need a comprehensive approach to school funding – so that local people do not have to contribute to school funds to keep the lights on. It didn't worry the 7% who sent their children to private schools, but it was certainly felt by every other parent. Starmer and Reeves need to make an immediate commitment to fund schools at least at the 2010 levels, adjusted for inflation by RPI. And they should then implement this funding.

Extra attention should be paid to SEN children and their funding restored to 2010 levels immediately. People only have one childhood and we should ensure that no child's education suffers as a result of austerity. This will help make sure that these children have a role to play in our society and the support they need.

Children's services should also be restored, including youth clubs and Sure Start – these children are our future. It must be done now – and there is nothing to stop us doing this.

Privatisation of council services, such as bin collection, was really just a con, and one that affected the people working on the waste services. Yes – the people transferred under *Transfer of Undertakings, Protection of Employment Act*, brought in to match EU regulations – no wonder the Tories wanted us to leave the EU – were protected and could hang on to their pensions. New employees were not given the same rights – and so many less well off people have been denied a local authority pension to save richer people money. There is no evidence that apart from cutting costs at the expense of the people working in the business, that the system is any more efficient – and of course the executives who run it have to be paid private industry extortionate rates while keeping down the salaries of the people actually doing the work.

As I wrote above, but want to emphasise, Sure Start must be brought back – destroyed with glee by Cameron and Osborne. Starmer and Reeves can make this commitment now.

Corruption should be pursued and the criminals taken to court, even if it is committed by the very rich. We need to establish a Corruption Commission, elected not filled with place people, and its role is not to do years of research, but to look at the most egregious examples now – and pursue them quickly and with the power to bring prosecutions bring them to justice.

Council housing must be built and to a better than Parker-Morris standard. This must be a commitment now – with actual money immediately given to councils to implement this policy. At the moment they are incentivising private companies to build more houses – and so-called *affordable* housing. In my area the cheapest houses are about £450,000, requiring a £45,000 deposit. I really don't know how ordinary people can afford to save that amount of money and live. If we can provide more social housing at subsidised rents, perhaps they will be able to save enough for a deposit. This is a long term commitment and will have no immediate benefits but it will be important.

The way the Department of Transport conducted rail franchising has to be investigated with the links of civil servants to various train companies part of that investigation. The cosy way that rolling stock is apparently owned by leasing companies should also be brought to an end. I don't know how that happened and it is certainly a way that private companies have leached money from the railways. Starmer and Reeves are committed to ending privatisation as the franchises fall – but the various tricks that the train operating companies (as they call themselves) used in gaining and giving up franchises should be exposed and immediately they should pay compensation where they gave up franchises early.

We should return rail fares to their cost in 1995, allowing for inflation, as a first step to making the fares more acceptable.

All appeals rejected by IPFAS should be immediately allowed and the money paid back by Govia – as it would be too expensive to go through every appeal that was disallowed, unless Govia wants to do that with a tight timetable and an independent company. The appeals were not heard by an *independent* appeals procedure and currently cannot be justified or known to be safe.

Philip Rutnam's role in covering up IPFAS's illegal position must be investigated and also the wilful blindness of Manzoni and Gray – and the role of Heywood exposed, even though he has died.

We must ensure that the National Health Service is restored to what it was before the Tory wreckers got hold of it and deliberately underfunded it and reduced what it does – do you know that once upon a time you could actually get a hernia operation without waiting interminably?

There must be an immediate focus on the national scandals that have ruined people's lives – and a pledge that within six months the Post Office scandal, the mad cow blood transfusion scandal, the Windrush scandal, the Grenfell cladding disaster and its aftermath, and the Chinook helicopter scandals, for starters, are dealt with and put to bed with proper compensation and, as important, the guilty people charged and taken to court. There is talk that there will be no criminal charges in the Post Office case till 2027. Absurd and we must insist that charges are brought as quickly as possible – and we need to bring a few people to trial immediately and not wait until we have all the guilty people in the ring.

Cleaning up this part of the dirty tricks practised by governments will give people faith that those in government are in touch with what people want and despite the fact that the rich and famous have perpetrated these acts, the rule of law prevails.

The executives of HSBC that were involved in the support of drug cartels have to be arrested and charged with the offences that they committed, helping the drug and people smugglers. We must find the people who failed to follow through to charge the executives and who let them off the hook, and see whether we can charge them with criminal neglect. We must also charge the regulators with misconduct who failed to do what was required when they knew what was going on.

If the BBC is right that the real culprit in the interest rigging scandal is the Bank of England, once again it isn't the Bank of England but senior people in the Bank of England and at the very least the BBC's allegations must be investigated and even if the people involved were senior figures in the Bank of England they must be prosecuted.

There must be no relaxation of the regulations brought in after the 2008 debacle which nearly destroyed our economy, because of the greed of the bankers. Letting bankers play with our economy to enrich themselves is like asking an arsonist if he would like some petrol.

We need an immediate examination of the HMRC sweetheart deals with major companies like Vodaphone as we know that Vodaphone won't have got a one-off special treatment so there will be many others such deals that benefit offshore corporates and their owners.

All the fines on people who are below the tax threshold who failed to fill in their tax return should at the very most no more than £200. Even the Tories agreed to this – and this can happen immediately and should as the legislation was already passed.

We need a new *Fairness Doctrine* to control all of the media – and it can be introduced immediately. This meant that there had to be two verifiable sources for every statement and a balanced view should be presented by the media company involved.

Levenson II – the recommendations made after the scandals of phone tapping and worse – must be enacted immediately to protect people from the gutter press and broadcasters.

In 2016 the EU was poised to bring in legislation that would have meant that individuals would have to declare all income, offshore and onshore, and pay the appropriate tax. Brexit conveniently allowed the rich to avoid having to declare their income and where their assets were, but we need action to ensure that we have this information.

We need to identify the profits made by the companies in the UK that offshore their profits to Ireland, including Apple, Google, Amazon and Starbucks, and therefore, apparently legally, *avoid* tax and then we must tax it at a proper rate. It is not possible to believe that the profits made by those companies here are as they state them – and there are many tricks used to increase costs and inflate the running expenses. In the 1980s, when I worked for Philips, a highly ethical Dutch international company, we all had to understand how to establish the real profits made in a country so that we could pay the appropriate local tax. For example, many companies use fraudulent transfer pricing – that is inflating the price of goods supplied from outside the country, so it looks like profits are lower than they actually are. Philips didn't allow this. This new tax take will be a major boost to tax revenues.

We need to ensure that the Investor-State Dispute Settlement clause in any trade deals is immediately repealed so that the corporates who fund our political parties cannot sue this government for, say, implementing measures against oil and gas companies.

The Freeports and Special Economic Zones should be immediately abolished and the UK's rule of law be applied across all parts of the country.

What Distillers did to the Thalidomide children and their families was appalling, and it was the Chief Executive and his board who were responsible for that. They were the ones who should have been pilloried for their inhumane and self-seeking failure to act. They were protecting their profits, their huge salaries and their bonuses and children were being treated with callous indifference. Those individuals have to be named and shamed even though most will be dead. It should be done so that current executives in companies faced with similar disasters know that they have to act ethically or be exposed as ghouls.

Brexit was a shambles and no-one was happy with the result. The Remainers were appalled that a non-binding referendum brought in by Cameron to try to keep the Tory Party unified was basically undermined by the lies and deceit of the Brexiters. Brexiters apparently think it didn't go far enough. This isn't an immediate priority but once people realised how bad it has been, they turned against Brexit. By directing people's justified anger at the EU the populists created a phantom – we can't do much about it but this government has to ameliorate the situation – and create a narrative that Brexit was a giant failure of government.

We also need to restore the foreign aid budget to 0.5% of GDP – to show humanity, to create a significant break with what populists want, and to show the vast majority of the UK population who believe in helping the poorest people in the world, that voting for Labour is a vote for humanity and fairness.

Wilful blindness, one of the great tools of the Civil Service and successive governments should become a crime.

As a last thought, no media company in the US is allowed to be owned by a non-American citizen – Murdoch was naturalised an American so he could add his malign spin and propaganda to US media and took over significant newspapers and developed Fox News, We should think about that for our country too.

Chapter 3

Further Actions to Create Hope, and Trust and Inspire People

If you are a two earner family and you are living on the edge all the time – what the Tories called *only just managing* – or if you are a single person paying 45% of your after tax income for a single room to live in, it is very difficult to have any hope. If you are reliant on benefits or a fixed pension, every day life will be a struggle.

These people are often in despair – for good reason – and are legitimately angry and I can see why the populists saying *we understand your problem and it's all the fault of the establishment* and, before that, *the EU, and we promise to help you* is immediately attractive, especially when they don't explain anything that they will do, like abolishing the NHS free at the point of contact.

There are three immediate steps that the government must take to renew the social contract with the people of this country and create hope and, as important, trust.

The first is to implement the policies outlined in Chapter 2 – especially the lowering of the VAT rate and the indexing of income tax thresholds – to show that the government actually understands the plight so many people are in. VAT is an enormous burden and we must focus on reducing it over time to 8% again. Putting more money in working people's hands and not taking so much from those who are not working will immediately show that the government understands and cares. It will restore hope.

According to right wing economists lowering taxes creates more wealth. In this case we will be lowering taxes and increasing the wealth of ordinary people – not creating billionaires.

The second is to create a commission to look at all the corruption of the last 20 years with a three month deadline and look at all the people who have profited at our expense and have got off scot free. It won't need to hear everything and examine everyone in detail. We know who profited from Covid contracts and who helped them. Identifying the HSBC executives should be straightforward – and they've already admitted their crimes and the Post Office scandal ought not to be a problem, after you've immediately compensated the sub-postmasters.

The third is to create a new ministry – currently we have a Ministry of Justice but now we must create a Ministry of Injustice dedicated to identifying the myriad of injustices that have occurred over the last 46 years, and as quickly as possible make sure that they are eliminated. This can focus on the scandals outlined in Chapter 1, but also the procurement scandal where Tory ministers gave special treatment to rich donors to the Tory Party, the Jenrick affair and even look at what Lady Porter was doing in the 1980s, under the protection of Thatcher. The danger is that governments will be able to slow this all down – so we must have tight timescales for all enquiries and resultant charges.

We must at the same time offer a vision of uniting people behind a strategy that will focus on helping ordinary people, taking into account all the many issues that are making their lives more difficult than they should be. Once we can again establish trust between the government and the people we can show people that we have a strategy and tactics that will help them.

We should also be aware that Artificial Intelligence (AI) is a significant factor and in the late 2020s it will be even more so, and it will have a major effect on our lives and employment. And it won't just be blue collar workers but many lawyers, accountants and other professionals will find that their working lives will be completely different. We have to have a vision that will show people that no matter what happens as a result of AI, the government will be there to ensure that peoples' lives can continue.

We should see that there is an immediate need to understand how a universal basic income could be brought in when so many workers are displaced by AI and other technologies. In the past when a new technology was introduced jobs were created. When banks introduced machine readable code on cheques – remember them? – there were predictions that this would remove the need for many bank workers, because no longer would people be required to process the cheques in the same way. In fact the banks ended up employing more people because suddenly they were able to have much more information about their customers and their banking and financial habits, and they employed people to handle data that had never been available before.

AI will not be the same. And we need to plan for it now. How can we pay for a *Universal Basic Income* is going to be a key issue in the late 20s and early 30s, as we transition to an entirely new world. I know that many people are already anxious about this – and we need to show them we have a plan.

There must be added focus on the climate crisis and no going back on commitments to ensure we become a carbon neutral country as soon as possible. We must create a new vision and world where we are committed to the future and not lecture people but inspire people with the prospect of the new jobs and opportunities creating a green future will bring.

The populists are supported by billionaires who usually remain in the shadows, and they have said that they will spend money and bank roll the Reform Party for example. They won't be doing that for the benefit of our people, you can be sure of that. Foreigners are not supposed to be able to give money to political parties, but we know they do and we know the malign effects of that. In fact our political parties are being increasingly bank rolled by rich people – that's probably one reason why Labour is so averse to bringing in a wealth tax.

This completely skews our political life without anyone seeing it and anyone doing anything about it. My proposal is that no donation over £1,000 can be made to any political party .in one year and all donations (I call them bribes because that is what they are mostly) must be registered and come from individuals not companies and unions. There will be squeals about this as both Tories and Labour are in receipt of large sums from rich people, but we need to take control of how political parties are funded. We must not allow our political life to become the plaything of billionaires and a slave to corporate needs, as it is in the USA.

If, like in America, a few rich people with hard right agendas fund political parties, then we see what happens, with Trump in power and the needs of corporations being the focus.

The current trend is to fine companies like Thames Water relatively large sums of money. But companies are actually run by people – think how refreshing it will be to see the fat cats in banking, in water companies, in hedge funds held to account – and held to account quickly.

We just haven't got time to waste, because the danger of populists using their malign tactics to take over this country because Starmer and Reeves are politically incompetent and pursuing the same old Tory policies, bounded in by the same old catchphrases and discredited concepts such as austerity, is real.

Starmer can save himself by remembering the promises he made to get the leadership of the Labour Party, by forgetting his ties to the rich and famous, by understanding the fury that the last 15 years have generated and why the fury is well justified, by forgetting his ties to a genocidal Israeli government in Gaza, and striking out in a new direction.

I doubt he can – but I don't rule him out.

If he carries on as he has started, we are doomed to a populist take over, the dismantling of our social structures and the removal of the rule of law. Every minority in this country – and that includes intelligent people – will be under threat. The time for action is now.

The clock is ticking.

Chapter 4

Observations

Starmer and Reeves, with the political sensitivity of a land mine came into office with a mandate for change and a 166 seat majority that could force through major changes. What did they do?

Much as expected, they hit the very people who had voted for them. They took away the extra heating allowance from most pensioners – and then means tested it – and next hit disabled people's benefits. A Labour Government hurting the poorest and people who are living hand to mouth! They refused to do anything about the two child benefit cap – and later promised to increase defence spending to 4%. They gave the populists exactly what they needed – a demonstration that both Labour and Tories are just the same, with the slight difference that no-one suspects Starmer of just being in it to enrich himself and his buddies.

Where was there any sense of fairness?

Where was there any recognition that people are justifiably angry?

All they did was to repeat that there was no money, that the Tories had left a black hole, and they were faced with difficult choices. What that always means is that they will do everything and anything except sort out all the injustices in our society while hurting ordinary people – and they hide behind the statement *there is no money*. Curious isn't it that if you want to bomb other countries and kill foreigners there is always plenty of money for that.

Difficult choices turn out to be anything that doesn't benefit the rich.

If Starmer and Reeves achieved anything they stoked the anger that most people feel, they undermined what little trust of politicians and government remained in the country and they squashed any chance of hope.

We just have to do something now – words don't matter as no-one believes a word any of them say. The only answer is action – immediate and comprehensive action.

The mainstream media is no longer so important – now we have tech billionaires mainly American, creating a cacophony of thousands of discordant voices, with no constraints and no ethics. But remember that the mainstream media still has a role, controlling the political narrative. You don't have to be a person who understands what Antonio Gramsci was writing, about the way the ruling class uses hegemony through the mass media to control thought, to know that the malign nature of the *Daily Mail,* the *Daily Express, The Sun, The Times* and the *Daily Telegraph* – with their witch hunts and their deflection and their hypocrisy – is not on the side of progressive people. Look what they were saying about Hitler in the 30s last century – they haven't changed. It may not be so important, but the BBC continually finds its lead from them and discusses matters within their framework. We can't actually drown them out but we can outflank them.

Once the Labour Government takes a new step towards actually helping people – there will be an enormous outcry from them that we can't afford this or that – which is why alongside our actions detailed in Chapter 2 we have to create a narrative that debunks these malign forces in our country, owned largely by offshore billionaires, and shows that they are nasty, committed to hurting people and full of hypocrisy.

Social media is a mess and controlled by offshore billionaires with little or no moderation or control over the filth that is generated in the apps, and all the conspiracy theories and denial of science and real knowledge. Some people still hope to use social media for progressive messages – and we shouldn't ignore it – but we cannot hope to use it too effectively, except to create echo chambers.

That is why it isn't the mainstream media, it isn't social media that must be our first target, although we cannot afford to ignore them.

We need action – quick decisive action – on most of the actions described in Chapter 2. If Starmer and Reeves can't do that, because of their connections and desire to remain within the cosy world of yesterday's elites making our lives intolerable, then the Labour MPs need to wake up and remember what can be done.

Remember Britain was on its knees in 1945 – it had fought a war which had cost lives, service and civilian, and used every bit of its wealth to do so. It was essentially bankrupt, but out of that mess, Atlee and his government created the welfare state. There was absolutely no money – but they created the new settlement and made sure there was no slump after the war – and they didn't spend the money on armaments but on orange juice – I'm old enough to remember National Health orange juice – and opportunities.

We need that determination now – and we need immediate action – and at the same time a narrative of hope and unity and a social conscience. There is nothing the populists hate more than hope, a vision of a better life – not the sado-populism that says your life is going to get worse (to support billionaires), but we are going to make life even worse for the minorities that we will pick on today so feel good about that. Think how many of the Maga cult are prepared to ensure a loss of Medicaid and higher shop prices for themselves because of tariffs if it means that *libtards* and *the woke* (you know the people with empathy and awareness) suffer more.

To understand our populists, think of all the populist self-styled Christians in the US who proclaim not love but hate, deny that Jesus was a Jew, and who have never read *the Sermon on the Mount*, or if they have read it, not understood it, or have understood it and don't believe it. Christians spouting hatred and forgetting *to love they neighbour*, forgetting the injunction to *suffer the little children to come unto me* and perverting its meaning into *make the little children suffer*, and finally the injunction to *help people* as the Good Samaritan did. That's how far populists are from having any empathy, any social conscience or any humanity.

Whatever else we do we have to have hope – based on concrete actions to make people's lives better.

As Obama used to say *Yes we can*. And we really can. Cut VAT immediately and see how people respond. Charge a few bankers who have already admitted their crimes with drug offences and see the difference. Restore our pride in our country like Atlee did at the point where there really was no money.

All it needs is determination, an understanding of how the economy can work for ordinary people – and a belief in doing the best for the people of this country – all of our people.

Populists feed on anger. We have to benefit from it by assuaging that anger.

My call is to Labour MPs – either get Starmer to change – or change Starmer for someone who understands and who has the political nous and will to become the new Atlee. People say Starmer has no charisma as if this is his biggest fault. Atlee was possibly the least charismatic Prime Minister we have ever had – but he got the job done. His ministers weren't cowed by antagonistic bankers, wealthy insurance companies, the BMA, the wealthy owners of the coal mines and the railways. They had a mandate for change. The Labour Government needs to act, be seen to act, explain what it is doing – and show the people that their lives can be improved by a Labour Government and that aspiration – including the aspiration that our children can have a better life, in a greener world, than the life that the billionaires hiding behind placemen will allow – is possible once again.

Create hope and restore trust by dealing with and eliminating what makes people angry and restore our sense of a society that is truly caring by implementing the programme identified here.

All the new Labour MPs are vulnerable to the populists if the Labour Government carries on in the way it is doing. As I wrote earlier, this has to be a great incentive to implement the change that Starmer and Reeves promised in their manifesto. The manifesto in this book will create trust, hope, and inspire people to trust government again and look forward to a better future.

Bite-Sized Books: A Modern Approach to Reading

Bite-Sized Books are a modern literary format designed to cater to the fast-paced lifestyle of today's readers. In essence, they are short, focused books or booklets—often ranging from a few thousand to around 15,000 words—that deliver clear, concise content on a specific topic. These compact reads are tailored for individuals who may not have the time or inclination to commit to lengthy volumes but still want to engage with thoughtful, informative, or entertaining material. The term "bite-sized" reflects both the brevity of the works and their ease of consumption, making reading more accessible and less intimidating.

The rise of Bite-Sized Books has been fuelled by changes in reading habits and technology. With the increasing use of smartphones, tablets, and e-readers, readers are more inclined to seek content that fits into short windows of time—during commutes, lunch breaks, or even while waiting in queuesl. Bite-Sized Books meet this demand perfectly. They allow readers to start and finish a book in one or two sittings, providing a sense of accomplishment and value without requiring a major time investment.

One of the strengths of Bite-Sized Books is their versatility. They can span a wide range of genres and subjects—from self-help and business advice to political commentary, fiction, poetry, and beyond. In nonfiction, these short books often focus on a single idea, trend, or argument, giving the reader a deep dive into the topic without unnecessary padding. In fiction, they can serve as novellas, short story collections, or serialised episodes that provide rich storytelling in a condensed form.

Bite-Sized Books are also a boon for writers, especially emerging authors or thought leaders looking to share insights quickly. The shorter format lowers the barrier to entry, allowing more people to publish meaningful content without the need for traditional publishing deals or lengthy production cycles. This democratises the writing space and leads to a greater diversity of voices and ideas.

Educationally, Bite-Sized Books can be particularly effective. They're often used in schools and training programs to introduce complex topics in a manageable form. Their brevity encourages reluctant readers to engage with material they might otherwise avoid, and their focused nature supports better retention and understanding of the content.

In a world of ever-decreasing attention spans, the concise nature of these books offers an alternative that respects the reader's time while still delivering meaningful content.

In summary, Bite-Sized Books represent an evolution in how we read and write. By condensing insight, narrative, or commentary into digestible formats, they make literature and knowledge more accessible to everyone. Whether for entertainment, education, or inspiration, they offer a smart, flexible option for modern readers.

Bite-Sized Books Ltd

Why not sign up to our mailing list here:

Why not browse our BOOKSHOP?

Find out more about Bite-Sized Books here:

Printed in Dunstable, United Kingdom

65807031R00057